Talitha Cumi: Get Up Little Girl!

Like Dust I Rise, Volume 1

Emma M Morobe

Published by Emma M Morobe, 2020.

While every precaution has been taken in the preparation of this book, the publisher assumes no responsibility for errors or omissions, or for damages resulting from the use of the information contained herein.

TALITHA CUMI: GET UP LITTLE GIRL!

First edition. August 31, 2020.

ISBN: 979-8230268376

Written by Emma M Morobe.

Table of Contents

Throw in the first stone

Created pure, without sin,

Pure as hyssop, white as snow,

Sent into a world that had been broken,

Fighting against everything and everything,

Fighting against all spirits that surrounded me.

I fought to keep pure,

I fought to stay on the path,

I fought to keep remembering,

Remembering the promises,

Remembering my mission,

Remembering my reason to live.

I tripped and fell,

It hurt me deeply,

I felt I was a failure,

I had failed my mission,

I had failed to keep true to the cause,

The world condemned me,

Made me feel worse,

Made me feel unworthy,

Made me feel unclean,

Made me look worse of a failure.

I went down to the one place I know,

I went down on my knees,

I looked to the heavens and prayed,

I poured out my heart for the Father,

I asked in the Son's name, in Jesus' name,

In Jesus' name I receive all that I ask,

In His name if I truly believe, I receive.

A response came from above,

I was counted as one of His children,

Forgiven for all my inequity and sin,

I was restored to my position,

All that the world had taken was returned,

My faith, my trust, my hope, my love,

All these were restored,

My mission was rewritten,

My strength rejuvenated.

Once again I believed,

Once again I walked tall,

I was free once more,

I knew now that the world was broken,

I knew that the broken people were further broken,

Further broken by others condemning them,

I knew now what to teach the world,

I taught mercy, I taught forgiveness,

We have all sinned, fallen away from our mission,

We all fall short of glory, we all need restoration,

I asked as I had once heard it asked on my behalf,

One who has never done wrong or sinned in their life,

Who ever is purest, let that one throw the first stone,

Throw it because you will never sin,

Throw it because you are perfect,

Throw it because you come from sinless blood,

Throw it because you are incapable of sinning,

Throw it because you never thought badly of someone,

Throw it because you think your sins are covered by the darkness,

Remember that nothing can be hidden from God,

Remember that all that is done in darkness shall come to the light,

Remember that each one shall be judged for their sins,

Judged for all of their sins, those visible and invisible.

Throw in the first stone,

If you have never sinned,

If you will never sin,

Judge others all you want,

Remember that God sees everything,

Just throw in that first stone.

All my sorrows within

When all that my pillow knows are my tears,

When all that my heart knows are my sorrows,

When all the my soul knows is my loneliness,

Will you still be there? Will you still care?

When all that my ears hear cause destruction within,

When all that comes to me rips me apart painfully,

When all that my eyes see shatters every part of me,

Will you still be by my side? Will you help me hold it together?

Will you still understand me when I cannot explain my tears?

Will you try to understand my actions when I try to hide from my sorrows?

Will you see the pattern when I run from my loneliness?

Will you understand me? Will you see my brokenness?

Will you listen when I tell you what I've heard?

Will you hear me or hear what I have also heard?

Will you see the pieces of me revealed before you?

Will you help me rebuild? Will you hear my heart?

When all that I have become is a pile of ashes,

Ashes from being burnt by that which I am yet to know,

Will you see me for what I truly am or will you be blinded still?

When I can no longer come back to life, will you be there?

Will you commit what is left of me to the ground or will you revive me?

My sorrows know no end, you can help yet you watch on,

My tears flow like a waterfall, yet they do not move your heart,

You standby and watch me die, yet you know I'm innocent,

You could save me, yet you wash your hands and stand with my accusers.

Will you still remember how I stretched my hands and called out for your help?

Will you remember the look in my eyes when death took my innocent soul?

Will you remember how I died at the words of their mouths?

Will you still pretend to be deaf and blind?

Blind to my pain, deaf to my cry but you see and hear,

You live in the shadow of those very ones that kill me,

Will you forget that you too can easily become a target?

Will you still think I'm guilty when your turn comes?

Your creation, Oh Potter

They crackle, they grumble,

No one hears it but me,

They are cracked and split,

No one sees it but me.

It beats low, it pounds hard,

No one feels it but me,

They flow, they sting,

No one feels it but me.

The walls that once protected,

The walls that held it all together,

The walls that kept it all in,

The walls that kept them all out.

The heart that once held me in place,

Its beating that was so constructed,

The tears kept at bay by false strength,

The waters I kept so hard from flowing.

I have always known, they never knew,

I always saw it; they were blinded from it,

I've always felt it; they never cared to feel it,

I've always heard it; their ears have never cared to hear it.

I'm broken, always have been.

They chose to see the my constructed strength,

They chose to ignore my moments of weakness,

They chose not to hear my cry for help.

Now they know, they see it too,

They can't feel it, they don't want to,

They can't hear my scream, their ears are closed,

It is clear that I'm broken yet no one can fix me.

I sit in darkness and cry;

My tear sacs have gone dry,

I then lift my eyes to you;

My everything, my creator,

Who else but You can I look to,

Who else but You can fix me,

Who else but You knows me,

Who else but You knows my life.

Oh my Potter, I am just clay,

Shattered clay, broken pieces,

Pieces of me are scattered,

They are too many to count.

Potter, Your creation is broken,

Potter, only You know how to fix me,

Lay me on your worktable and work on me,

You know all that they don't, all that I don't.

Pieces belonging to places in me,

Places I never knew existed but You did,

As you piece me back together, I be patient,

Once You are done I will be whole again.

You Woman!

This world was designed to disappoint you,

It was not designed to uphold you

Or to encourage you,

It was not designed to be friendly towards you.

This world was created for you,

It was created beautiful like you

To enable you to be the best you can be.

This world was designed by man,

This world was created by God,

A designer only knows what they think

But a creator knows beyond current thoughts.

Those who designed it to fit their thoughts don't know you,

They assume they do, they design theories such as biology,

Theories meant to try and understand you,

Theories meant to define you.

They designed customs and imposed them on you,

They put themselves high above you,

They told you that you are nothing without them,

They oppressed your ancestors and now you,

They think they have you all figured out.

The one that created it didn't set limits on what you can do,

The creator didn't put you in a box and imprison you,

The creator simply allowed you to be free,

Free to think, free to speak,

Free to evolve, free to compete,

Free to engage and free from restraints.

The creator knows your abilities, even those you are not aware of,

You were created to be greater, created for better,

No theory designed and shaped by man can ever define you,

You are a unique being that cannot be boxed,

You are a powerhouse of thoughts, ideas and expressions,

The only one who has you figured out is your creator.

Get up and design, design a world that is true,

Don't design to avenge yourself or your ancestors,

Design to reconcile the oppressor with the oppressed,

Design to open their eyes,

Design to help those that come after you,

Design so that your creator can be proud,

Design to heal.

This world can be designed to understand you,

This world can be designed to accommodate you,

It can be shaped to allow the existence of both,

Both you and them.

Stand up and stand tall,

Don't conform to their ways,

Stick to the truth,

Stick to fairness,

Stick to humanity.

By Mercy

When they thought I was dead,

When they thought I was out,

When they thought I was weak,

When they thought I had no way out,

And they thought I was finished.

When the walls were closing in on me,

When I could not breathe anymore,

My lungs crushing in and air rushing out,

The sun was going down on my hope,

Despair and gloom came over me,

And I felt my life was doomed.

Tears flew from my eyes day and night,

My heart was in a million pieces,

Life was no longer important to me,

Nothing mattered, nothing made sense,

Death was becoming hopeful,

And darkness rejoiced at my pain.

A new day dawned,

A revival came to my soul,

At the Father's feet I cried,

In the Son's name I asked,

By the Spirit I received.

Since then His mercy has not left me,

His mercy touched my heart,

His mercy changed my mind-set,

His mercy restructured my life,

And by this mercy I survive.

I believe now,

I believe that His mercies endure forever,

I believe that it is by this mercy that we receive grace,

I believe that it is by His mercy that I've been forgiven,

And it is by this mercy I shall find peace.

Still my beloved

I still cannot comprehend you,

I still wonder if you are really here,

I still ask myself why I have you,

I still wait for you to turn from me.

I still wonder why you captivate me,

I still get lost in your smile,

I still think that you won't stay,

I still fear what could go wrong.

You are still that which my mind cannot understand,

You are still an extraordinarily human being,

You still ask me questions that I ask myself of you,

You still make me feel safely lost.

Your smile still rescues me from sadness,

Your sadness still makes me want to cry,

Your arms still tell me I'm safe,

Your actions have taught me to trust your arms.

Your heart I cannot see but I've seen is that you are here,

Your eyes have a tendency of saying thing beyond your lips,

You have no idea why I'm here, I have no idea why you are still here,

You have heated me up when it's cold, I only hope I have done the same.

When I fail to hold it together, it is you who lifts me up,

When I go crazy, it is you who calms me down,

In all things, you can handle me; you have seen my mind,

You can subside my fears, you can strengthen my hopes.

You gave me open access to your mind; unknowingly so did I,

I learn daily how you shift; unknowingly so do you regarding me,

You do not believe that you are my prince charming; I don't believe I found you,

Time is kind, life is cruel; knowingly and unknowingly we journey to the unknown.

Your arms told me to trust you, your actions taught me to,

My lips tell you what I feel, my heart hopes my actions show you,

My mind tells me I'm in too deep, my heart tells me to act gingerly,

My soul is lost in you, it knows only that I am safe all-round and it trusts carelessly.

Mountains that used to be too high to climb have become a joyous challenge,

Fears that had not real roots have died, hope has become stronger,

The thoughts I never had have begun to visit my mind,

Thoughts of actual happiness, that fairy-tale I dream about.

A part of me still tells me I'm going to wake up,

Wake up to the horror of life, where you don't exist,

Wake up to the horror of reality, where what we have is unreal,

A part of me tells me to keep sleeping.

When my eyes first flashed differently on you, I rebuked them,

When my brain started thinking differently, I silenced it,

When your lips agreed with my brain and mind, I was shocked,

Knowingly I agreed, held your hand to walk this unknown path.

My mind still can't comprehend you, you amaze me still,

My heart still awaits shutting you out, you make no mistake,

Am I crazy? Am I infatuated? This isn't a crush anymore,

I am way beyond being infatuated, I'm in love, that unfair state.

In love with you my beloved,

I still beat around no bush with you,

Honesty feels like the only key for me,

I hope someday I will comprehend you.

Time has passed since I called you beloved,

Things have happened since I called you beloved,

Through all these, we have not faded away,

After all this time you are still my beloved.

Restoration

A river once flowed,

Now only a canyon remains,

Hot and dry the soul has become.

When shall love rain?

When shall peace flow?

Is the river ever going to flow again?

Oh, what a pity,

I await the return of joy,

Hopefully the day is near.

Death of pain

Ancient words lost not forgotten,

Words that I once accepted,

These very words that my heart never received,

My ears heard them, my head processed them,

But my heart never got the message.

A glimpse of you, a shadow from the dead,

A glimpse of memory, a glimpse of life,

They resounded once again, those words,

Those ancient words that you said,

You said them but you did not mean them.

My head had long processed them,

My ears had heard them,

I thought I had accepted,

That shadow, that glimpse,

The reappearance of your face.

The reappearance of your physique,

A structure I had never thought to ever see,

A structure that awakened my heart,

A structure that awakened the pain,

My heart realized it had not received.

My heart had not received your message,

It had not yet processed your forgiveness,

It had not yet received word from you,

It had only lied to me and said you were forgiven,

My own heart told me a lie.

Because of you, you made my heart lie to me,

The very part of me that had been true and real,

Your failure to send a word corrupted it,

My mind decided without my heart's consent,

You were forgiven, the pain was erased.

You were erased along with it,

How could you teach my heart to lie?

How could forgiveness mean so much?

Why was a missing apology accepted in my head?

The death of this pain will come once a word from you is received.

Hold me

Hold me, hold me tight and not let go,

For the night is near,

And the coldness looming,

Hold me in your reassuring arms,

Let me feel your warmth all around me.

Hold me tight to your chest so I fear not,

Let the twinkle in my eye cause a spark in your heart,

Your heartbeat sends a phenomenal beat to mine,

It makes a song that reassures me that the night will pass,

A song that reassures me that in your arms I shall not get frosty.

Your breath convinced me that I was safe,

It told me that your arms would not break me,

It told me that your heart treasured me,

It told me that the fire would never grow cold,

Safe and sound I was when you held me.

But alas, I flew through the air and hit the ground,

Your hands grew cold and froze around me,

They shattered to pieces and broke me in the process,

There was no future anymore, tomorrow was gone,

I was warm while you went cold.

I lied to myself or did your arms lie to me?

The warmth of your arms was a placebo,

The safety that overcame me was an illusion,

Did I life to myself or did you grow cold?

Hold me one last time so I can know the truth.

Tweety bird

Oh tweety bird,

Why are you so full of fear?

Why do you not do what you long for?

You were born for this, why do you fear it?

Your wings may be small but they will carry you,

They will carry you to the place you so desperately long to be,

They may look weak but they were designed for this,

Do not fear, you were born for this,

Spread your wings, start flapping them,

Jump off out of the nest and into the air,

The wind will be there beneath you, it will carry you,

The wind will help fulfil your longing.

Tweety bird, courage is not easy,

It is much harder than fearfulness,

Fear blocks you from being fulfilled,

Fear tells you that you can't,

Fear tells you that you will fall,

It reminds you of that time you tried and failed,

Fear only wishes for you not to try,

Fear ensures that you only desire and not accomplish,

Courage says you can, it says you will,

Courage tells you that you are wiser,

It tells you that you have learnt from past failures,

Courage tells you that your wings are strong enough.

Go ahead tweety bird,

Spread those wings, flap them,

Jump out into the air, feel the wind beneath you,

Remember what you learnt from your fall,

Remember to keep flapping your wings,

Remember to rest and glide when the time comes,

You are more courageous than you realise,

Don't let fear tell you that you can't,

Don't let memories paralyse you from trying,

This is a new day tweety bird, a new wind blows,

A new sun shines; even you have new feathers,

Fly tweety bird, you were born for this.

Talitha koum!

TALITHA!!!!!!

TALITHA KOUM!!!!!

Further away she kept drifting,

The louder I shouted, the further she became.

Tears rolling down my face,

The feeling of failure setting in,

Smaller her shadow became,

Further she went.

TALITHA!!!!!!!!!

TALITHA koum!!!!!

Talitha koum!!

Into the darkness she drifted,

My gifts were of no use on that day,

My faith was distorted on that day,

My hope turned off like a candle in the wind,

Felt like I was waiting for a bus in the middle of an ocean,

She never even turned to look at me,

She never even heard my voice,

Talitha koum, I said.

Like wet soap she slipped from my hands,

Numb and rubbery my arms felt,

Guilt passed through me like lighting,

I had done it; I had allowed her to crash like an egg,

A scream from deep inside reached my ears,

Nothing more mattered, it was my fault,

For a long time I thought it was my fault,

She hit the floor like a domino,

Talitha! White as snow were her eyes,

The couch was no comfort for her,

Little red lines decorated her snow white eye balls,

Panting like one who had run a marathon was she,

She was fighting to gasp some air,

"Talitha koum!" I said.

Talitha koum!
Jesus had said it, on my lips is was empty,
She drifted further towards the voice,

"Talitha koum" it said, calmly and gently so,

"Talitha koum" I said, trembling and filled with fear,

The maiden had been called to awaken,

To me she was to awaken and relieve me of my fear,

To relieve me of my guilt, pain and terrible fear,

To Him she was to awaken and leave behind her pain,

Leaving behind all the sorrows of life, all the sadness around,

Her eyes open that side and closed this side,

Her heart started beating normally once again,

She breathed like nothing had ever happened.

"Talitha!!!" I screamed from the top of my lungs,

She awoke, happy and refreshed.

The louder my screams became, the further away she went,

Peace had reached her at long last,

She was no longer walking in the blazing desert sun,

No longer would thorns pierce her naked feet,

The Master had spoken, the maiden had woken,

"Talitha koum" He had said, effective it was,

Like a breeze coldness filled the room,

Darkness covered the sky; it rained like never before,

The sun had fallen from the sky, the light was gone,

For us it was the end, for her it was a new beginning,

Everlasting peace and everlasting longing began that day,

Someday the Lord shall call out again,

"Talitha koum" shall He say,

That day the light will be restored,

Hope and love shall reign once again in our land.

Talitha koum.

So I can know who I am

You walked with me all my entire life,

You were always there to catch me when I fall,

You never left me but I drifted away from you,

You never gave up on me but I gave up on you,

You always trusted me but I could not trust no more.

Father I need your help,

need to learn to come back to you,

need a map,

need to find my way back home,

need your hand,

So I can reach out to you,

Father I need to know you,

So I can know who I am,

need to be with you,

So my soul can be free.

walked to find my way back home,

fell too many, many times,

And every time you reached out for me,

I took your hand but somehow I got lost,

I found myself in the hands of the devil,

I did not know, I thought I was still with you,

You opened my eyes and showed me the truth,

I could not believe I had drifted so far,

Now I need to come home,

Open my heart and my mind and my eyes.

Father I need your help,

I need to learn to come back to you,

I need a map,

I need to find my way back home,

I need your hand,

So I can reach out to you,

Father I need to know you,

So I can know who I am,

I need to be with you,

So my soul can be free.

Ready or Not, Here I come.

Inspired by those who aspire to achieve

I am a force to be reckoned with,

I take my time to observe before I hit the road,

Patience instilled so deep in me that I surprise myself with it,

I never rush even when I'm being fast.

Fruits of the spirit take time to grow,

My first being patience the next to be unveiled,

Anointed to be great and yet at times I feel small,

Impatient within patience yet it is His time that counts not mine,

Some mornings I don't wanna get out of bed

but my eyes open because it's His will that I live yet another day.

Ridding like a Ferrari I'm coming for my destiny,

It was set into motion before I was given breath,

No man can stand before me and I can not run from it either,

Stop me and you fall, I run from it and I find myself running right back towards it,

Who are you to change me, who am I to run because it is He who holds it in His hand.

Close your eyes and open your ears,

Can you hear that?

Those are my footsteps, coming towards success,

They said I'd never make it, that I'd end up in the gutter,

Well, see me now, here I stand,

Alive by His grace, His will and not yours,

My life that He gave His for.

Smug faced crowds cheering me on in victory,

Turning your backs on my struggle,

Guess what I know now?

I can loose man but I can't loose God.

Open your eyes because here I come,

Like dust I rise, fierce like a tornado,

Coming for what is mine,

Look up world because my day has come,

Your words, your walls have been demolished,

Ready or not, here I come.

Dead I shall remain

They pronounced me dead on arrival,

My eyes were still open,

My heart still beating strong,

My hand extended out to greet them

But I was dead to them.

In small doses, with tiny whispers,

Little by little their poison got into my blood stream,

Green blood, yellow eyes and purple eyes I got,

Still trying to let them hear me, to know me,

A corpse can only been seen nothing more.

Realizing I was alive, shivers went through them,

Scheming and plotting arose from nearby,

Slowly pictures were painted, articles distributed,

Once again headlines pointed to me,

Simple old me was portrayed complicated like the Davinci code.

Dead on arrival I was declared,

Out in the cold loneliness I was placed,

A flash of light shone, a voice spoke to me,

Life was breathed into me, plotting and scheming returned,

My joy was taken like a rainbow vanishing from the sky.

Recommendations to new happiness brought forth,

My idea of happiness tossed out, their joy became their pain,

Fear roamed their heads, my mouth never uttering a word,

They feared what I had come to know but I was never them or like them,

They pronounced me dead on arrival and dead I shall remain.

For in my death I can haunt; haunt them like their fear of my lips,

In my death I shall be feared, for they saw me dead but know I too can see,

Oh, my dear eyes. What hast thou seen that thy lips shall utter?

They think the carpet shall hide them, poor poltroons!

They do not know a dust storm rises when the carpet is lifted.

Dead; being dead is bliss, a blessed bliss,

In my death I haunt, my shadow spreads fear,

My eyes see, my ears hear and I know everything,

My lips sealed, for I do not engage in deformation of character,

Dead I shall remain; my resurrection shall come with glory and victory.

Awaken!

Not dead but sleeping,

Unaware of all that is around you,

Deaf to the voices surrounding you,

Can't hear all that is being said against and about you,

Mute and can't speak up for anyone,

Can't even speak for yourself,

Blind and can't see anything at all,

Not even the plots against you.

You awake and yet there's no change,

Your ears can't hear what they need to,

Open but no sound travels through them,

Your mouth can't say what it needs to,

Only a senseless noise comes out of you,

Your eyes can't see what they need to,

They are open but not perceiving.

O maidens, awaken!

Awaken from this plastic life you live,

Awaken from this darkness you are in,

Awaken from the ignorance that you are in,

Awaken to the troubles around you,

Awaken to the deceit around you,

Awaken and live in the reality around you,

Awaken to the sounds around you,

Awaken to the beauty around you.

O young women, awaken!

See the world as it is,

Full of love, joy, peace and sorrow,

Full of disappointments and opportunities,

See yourselves for what you are,

Beautiful, intelligent, inspirational,

Loving, caring, resilient and strong.

Awaken princesses, daughters of God,

Love yourselves and others as God has loved you,

Take charge with power and authority as given through Christ Jesus,

Awaken to the true you, put the potential in you to use.

This too shall pass

Dry as the desert they have become,

Cracked like the bottom of a scorched river,

Hot like a volcano my head has become,

Like they were sprayed with chillies my eyes feel,

My pillow is buffed up with all this saltiness,

But I know that this too shall pass.

My ears hear of it again, and again,

Reminded constantly of it I am,

Hurt drives into my heart like a knife,

A knife that once cut loose those ropes,

Those ropes that imprisoned me and denied me freedom,

That same knife today pierces my heart mercilessly,

Bringing me more pain that it would have had it left me imprisoned.

Like a river my pain flows,

The prophet had said justice would flow like a river

But to me pain and sorrow flows like a river.

"Strong waters will not take you" a prophet once said

But just a cup seeks to drown me,

I am as low as the last pond on earth.

My tear sacks have run dry,

My eyes hurt, look red and cracked,

My cheeks have cracked lines where my tears used to run,

My head hurts from all this sorrow and constant flow of tears,

I have reached the point where I can't cry no more.

This too shall pass,

All the sorrow,

All the pain,

All the humiliation,

All the fear,

All the doubt,

All these emotions that pull me down,

All these different stories that they tell,

All these reminders of my past,

All these lies and misconception,

All that is against my better tomorrow,

All the negativity surrounding my life,

All these shall come to pass,

Nothing last forever, no matter how good or bad,

And so this too shall pass.

Dancing with the darkness

Cold and alone, alone and cold,

The crowd surrounded me,

Their smiling faces gazed upon me,

Yet the darkness kept coming for me,

It feared not what would happen with a crowd around.

Surrounded yet alone, closer the darkness came,

Perfect images of the one who created me stood before me,

All dressed up like mannequins they all were,

Meaningless conversations that helped me not,

Amid them the darkness stood.

Pretentious smug crowd smiling and chatting,

The darkness reached out and held my hand,

Glued up in their own filth, they saw nothing,

They hid behind paintings of others and their own makeup,

They saw not as the darkness held my hand with a cunning smile.

The darkness caressed my arm, pulled me closer,

On the dance floor he held me close to his chest,

No one noticed me slip away, blind crowds don't see,

Safer in his arms I drifted, I saw a new side of him,

The darkness was not what it had always been branded as.

The darkness was warm, his arms were reassuring,

Never before had anyone been so real and close to me,

He touched my heart; he brought me to life,

The darkness became my lifeline, my stronghold,

In the distance I saw the light, I wonder of its relevance to me now.

Shadows of me

All cried out,

The desert is moist compared to my tear sacs,

After a billion tears have escaped my eyes,

After tissues have ran from my presence,

After reasons to cry have vanished,

An eco remains.

The eco of who I used to be sounds in my ears,

The shadow of who I was lingers alongside me,

All that remains is this empty shell,

A shell that needs to be filled once again,

Once again I find myself searching.

Some look at me and see something,

I look at myself and see a reflection,

A reflection of something long gone,

They say there is a bright tomorrow ahead,

I see only darkness and despair.

Dear love...

Lost while trying to find you,

Was it even proper for me to go looking?

Was it mine to search for you?

Would I have gotten lost if I hadn't tried to find you?

Fear set over me,

I wanted to turn back

But I kept going bravely,

I hoped and prayed that I'd find you.

Bruised and blue I became,

Confusion overtook me,

Torn apart I bled,

To pieces my heart shattered.

Patience!

Was it even worth it?

Do memories even count?

What a journey it was.

Bravely I set out,

Not yielding I went on,

Thought I found you,

I called out to you.

Alas, it was just a shadow,

A shadow that looked real,

A shadow I mistook for you,

A shadow that quickly faded.

Without anything to catch me I fell,

I hoped that the shadow was you,

I hoped that it was real, that it would catch me,

Oh my! How the ground hurt.

The ground caught me,

The shadow disappeared,

Broken pieces all over,

Now I glue them back together.

From these pieces a new thing shall come,

From these pieces a lesson has been learnt,

From these pieces I shall rebuild anew,

It was never my place to even go looking.

I will stay right here,

The real you will come for me,

When you are ready you will arrive,

You will find me on your own.

I do hope you will find me waiting,

I hope I will still have faith in you,

I hope I will still be wishing for you,

Most of all I hope you won't be a shadow.

Caught in the love of the darkness

For long the darkness loomed upon me,

Looming at me from a distance,

Looming me into a place of safety,

I ran and ran, into a corner I ran,

Alas I didn't know this was exactly where it wanted me.

The darkness whispered to me,

It uttered words that made me believe,

It made me believe in its goodness,

It made me believe in its strength,

Like putty in its hand I became.

Like a fly caught in a trap I was,

The darkness kept whispering sweet nothings to me,

Sweet nothings that left me blind and paralyzed,

No movement came from me like a fly in a spider's web,

My hands made out the shape of the darkness.

I learnt to love the darkness,

It was different from the light,

It never judged me but pushed me to an introspect,

I saw myself anew; I saw pieces of me I never knew of,

I saw my naked self in the reflection of its eyes.

Caught in the rediscovery of myself,

I missed the greatness of the light,

Distracted by the kindness of the darkness,

It allowed me to be myself without deviation,

The judgemental light had no place in my life.

The light had put me on trial for my mistakes,

The darkness encouraged me to learn from my mistakes,

The light had told me I'm not good enough or worthy of it,

The darkness taught me to think and strive to be better,

The light was cold towards me, the darkness believed in me.

Caught in the sweet love the darkness showed me,

Caught in the kindness and care shown by the darkness to me,

The light slipped my mind and memories, it slowly faded,

The darkness consumed me wholly and wholeheartedly I submitted
to it,

Truer a love had I never seen expressed till I got caught in the love of the darkness.

The call

From deep within me I heard a cry,

A cry so loud it awakened me from my sleep,

She screamed so loud that I was shaken,

Shaken roughly out of my sleep,

She cried for freedom.

I heard her say 'I'm calling out to you, come'

I searched day and night,

Searched from the east to the west,

From the north to the south,

Within crowds and nations,

In the eyes and thoughts of others,

Yet I could not find her.

Finally I went down to the one place,

The one place my mother had taught me,

There I heard the voice clearly,

She said to me 'you have come, now listen'.

I silently knelt there and then I heard it,

It was the calmness of the place,

Her screams were no more,

In the silence I heard a voice.

It was the Father, the Lord,

Saying 'I have called you, you have heard',

'Before you were conceived I knew you'

I knew all that you would become'

'I knew that life would be as it has turned out'

'Come to me, be free, be still, be yourself'

'I chose you before you knew me'

'I loved you before mountains had foundation'

'You are mine, my daughter, my servant'

'Abide in me and I in you'.

I heard, I searched, I looked, I found,

I found love and nurture,

It was, is and will be the call,

Hear it, search for it,

Find it and come for it,

The Lord is calling.

Phoenix

In the last days, I fell out of the sky,

Like a shooting star I came crashing down,

In the last days, I burnt out,

I had given all of me and all of my strength,

On my last day, I burnt to ashes,

There was nothing more I could give.

I had lived my life,

Fought a lot, shed tears,

Laughed a lot, had joyous moments,

I had loved and hated,

Been vengeful and forgiving,

This was the end of me,

To my enemies it was joyful,

To my loved ones it was painful,

To me it was just the end.

My creator had not yet finished with me,

I was drained and irreparable in my own eyes,

But to my creator knew I still had a purpose,

My creator knew it was not yet over,

My God decided it was time for restoration in my life,

A new beginning was in the thoughts of my creator.

From the ashes I rose,

Ashes that they had already cast off,

They had already said 'ashes to ashes',

Yet my creator restored me,

Turned my black dark ashes into a black diamond,

A black diamond I am,

Reborn from ashes like a phoenix,

Rejuvenated, stronger, tougher and better.

From the ashes I rise,

Never to be killed again, never to die out again,

Reborn with full strength and vision,

Restoration in its fullness,

My enemies frown at me,

My loved ones smile at me,

I smile at my creator with a thankful heart,

I'm wiser now, stronger and alive,

A phoenix I am.

The darkest hour

In the darkest hour of night,

I heard you calling out my name,

In the darkest hour of night,

I saw you falling to the ground,

In the darkest hour of night,

I saw you walking on upon a cloud,

In the darkest hour of night,

I knew I had lost you forever,

I knew I would never see you again.

In the deepest darkness I heard your voice,

I heard how you needed me to be there,

So close yet so far I was,

So blind with vision I was,

My hands tied on my back,

I couldn't reach out to you,

Up high upon a cloud I saw you walk,

Its silver lining shining so bright,

Swiftly it drifted, taking you away.

In the darkest hour of the night,

They came and took you away,

Warnings had been sent but

None of us ever understood,

In the brighter hours you touched our souls,

In that darkest hour you ripped our souls,

In our darkest hour we hoped for your return,

In your darkest hour you never looked back,

In that darkest hour we failed to say goodbye.

Torn but in one piece

It took guts to go that far,

Never looking back or around I trusted,

Down went my defences and I stood exposed,

You took me like a storm and I was blown away like a leaf.

I fell so deep into the black hole,

So deep I couldn't see the light,

Blinded by your cunning voice,

Stolen by your sweet lips.

When the road ahead opened up for me,

When I thought everything was falling into place,

One thing rolled out; the idiot in you rolled out,

The coward you are inside surfaced.

I pity you; I pity your tiny mind,

I pity you because you weren't man enough,

Not man enough to talk things through,

Not man enough to notice that I'm a lady,

A genuine lady with understanding.

Torn apart I lay in bed and cry; tears keep rolling down,

I pity myself for being foolish,

Foolish enough to think you were real,

I saw a new beginning in what was not even there,

I planned my life around a shadow; the shadow of you.

In one piece I shall rise,

When my tears have turned to dust and I cant cry over you anymore,

When your name no longer brings me tears,

When your name has become ordinary to my ears,

When you are no longer part of my memories,

When you finally die within me,

The day I lay you to rest in my mind.

Diamonds always come out of ashes and coal,

I guess you were part of the ashes,

I'm yet to find my lump of coal,

The lump in which my diamond is based,

I am the first piece of my diamond,

Thought you'd be the last.

In one piece I have risen from my death bed,

The place where many wished me to be

while you pretended you wanted me elsewhere,

remembered that it is not your power that keeps me alive,

It is God, my beating heart and the air I breathe,

In one piece I am once again,

We brought nothing into this world

and we take nothing out of it,

To my life you brought nothing but

You took a part of me and tore it apart.

Deep cuts take time to heal,

I'm healing,

Tomorrow you'll be gone,

I'll still be here; in one piece.

To my soul

Cry my soul, cry,

Let tears drop from your eyes,

Cry my soul, cry,

For it is not a sign of weakness,

but a sign of healing.

Shout my soul, shout,

Shout from the top of your voice,

Shout my soul, shout,

For it is not a sign of insanity,

but a sign of relieving your frustrations.

Tremble my soul, tremble,

Let vibrations got through your body,

Release the pain and anger,

Shake it all off,

Heal from within.

No gloom will ever befall you again,

Stand tall and strong,

Like a willow, you have been refreshed,

Like a fire, you have been renewed,

You are stronger, you are healed.

Reminiscing on shadows

Reminiscing on shadows,

The shadows of who we used to be,

Caught up in pain of sorrow and loss,

The loss of our former selves,

Pain brought us together.

In each other's arms we found comfort,

In these arms we were not lost but found,

In each other's eyes we were new,

We didn't know the other's former life,

In our own eyes; we had failed, we were shattered.

We took risks, we waged war,

A war that would release us from our prisons,

Prisons that kept us reminiscing on shadows,

The shadows of our past greatness and triumph,

The shadows that made us blind to each other.

Between us passionate flames burned,

A blaze that would set our paths to glorious calamity,

You were my drug; I never wanted to be without you,

I was your fuel; you said I made you want to do better,

So blind to each other's plight yet so deeply infatuated we were.

The expression of our pain was so beautiful,

Our blindness called it love; our bodies called it remedy,

The ecstasy numbed our pain and gave us hopeful hallucinations,

Hallucinations that you conquered the world and I conquered my fears,

These hallucinations escorted us to fearlessness,

Fearlessly we stoop at the top of the mountain,

The mountain that shone light upon our shadows,

Finally we learnt to let go of the haunting shadows,

Finally our blindness to each other's plight was lifted,

The passionate flames subsided and the ecstasy wore off.

Without ecstasy there were no hallucinations,

The passionate flames had nothing to do with us anymore,

Our need for each other was no more; we were fearless,

You were on path to conquer the world; to reign over all,

I had conquered my fears and was ready to take on the world.

Without blindness we saw the real person,

Hungry for a better world we both were,

No more reminiscing on the shadows of who we once were,

We are now looking at the projections of who we can become,

Engraved in stone and written in the stars we will be.

Reminiscing on shadows held us back,

Ecstasy brought us a helpful escort,

Fearlessly we stand now on separate paths,

No longer infatuated but empowered,

We take on the world from different corners.

Now I reminisce on what we used to have,

That volcanic passion that almost killed us,

That volcanic passion that taught us to survive,

The volcanic passion that made us stronger,

Reminiscing on hallucinations that brought hope.

Reminiscing on good portions of the expression of our pain,

Wondering if the hallucinations were all there was,

Ecstasy can lie but human physique fails to lie,

Shadows gone by, reality nakedly stands before us now,

The truth remains that we are cured and going for the world.

Oh Darkness!

Oh Darkness!

What hast thou done unto me?

The light keeps calling out my name

But it is with thee that I feel most at home.

Oh but Darkness; I need thee,

My tears never fall to the ground in your presence,

In your presence my pain is never in vain,

Your words are ever so encouraging and reassuring.

Darkness, my beloved,

Am I hopelessly lost with you?

So secure you make me feel,

Brave in your hand am I.

Oh Darkness, the light looks beautiful,

Like a piece of ice it's transparent,

It hides nothing and yet it looks cold,

With you I feel warm though I can't see through you.

I love that you care Darkness,

I love that you refuse to leave my sight,

The light that reaches out its hand for me has left me once before,

It has made and broke countless promises while you have kept all yours.

Oh Darkness, what would I be without you?

So many times the grave has called out to me,

It has waved its hand at me but your hand has kept me safe,

Your hand has guided me back to life countless times.

Oh but Darkness why do I need you so?

Why is it that without you I fall apart?

What is it about you that fastens pieces of me together?

What is it that you provide that light can't provide?

I remember when the light tried to steal me from you,

I remember the look on your face; you had no sign of worry,

You knew that I was yours; confidently you stood by and watched,

With all my might and strength I clung to your warmth.

Oh Darkness, don't ever leave me,

I need you more than the air I breathe,

Don't ever leave me out in the cold light,

Cover me under your hand, never let me go.

This time was the last

So many times I try to believe in you,

So many times you have let me down,

Time and time again I believe that you will change,

I keep on believing that things will get better,

With every promise you make, my hope in you is restored,

It is restored like the innocence of a child,

A child that has never had their heart broken,

A heart that still believes in the goodness of the world,

The very goodness that your actions have stripped me of,

Yet I have a strange faith in you and your promises,

The promises that you've broken so many time before,

The promises that filled me with hope only to leave me shattered,

Shattered into a million pieces that you were never there to help pick up,

Alone I collected the pieces of me and glued them together again,

When I'm in one piece you arrive to give me your hope,

My desperation for a better day gets a hold of me and I find myself believing in you,

Like a fool I believe in your new promises,

I believe in them as though you have never broken them before,

I believe in them as though you are not the same as before,

Like an innocent child I look forward hopefully,

Patiently I wait upon you to deliver on your promises,

Once again I shatter to a million pieces at your failure to deliver,

You fail once again to deliver what you promised,

So many times I've tried to believe in you,

So many times you've let me down and you've left me shattered,

Once again I believed and now alone I pick up the pieces,

Once again you've let me down; this time was the last.

Ταλιθά κοῦμι